Minute Help Guides Presents:

A Newbies Guide to iPod Classic

SOME PEOPLE ONLY HAVE A FEW MINUTES TO SPARE

Minute Help Guides

Minute Help Press

www.minutehelp.com

Cover Image © Jaimie Duplass - Fotolia.com

Table of Contents

Introduction

While there are half a dozen newer iterations of the iPod on the market today, none of them can really compete with the iPod Classic in the one arena that matters most to music junkies: space. With as much as 160GB worth of content right in your pocket, the iPod Classic is the one device in Apple's mobile ecosystem that can deliver your entire library to your fingertips.

This guide will take you through the ins and outs of the iPod Classic. From managing your library of content with iTunes to discovering your new favorite podcasts, this guide will tell you what you need to know, saving the fluff for people who have time to waste.

Ready to get started? Let's go!

Part One: Introducing iPod Classic

The iPod Revolution: A Short History

In the prehistoric days before ubiquitous computers and DVD Burners (the 1970s), The LP record was king. For the uninitiated among you, LP records were 12 inch round discs with little grooves in them. They were pretty much the only way people consumed music at home for much of the 20th century. LPs looked like this:

The great thing about LPs, at least for the music industry, was the expense. Difficult to manufacture and even more difficult to steal, consumers had basically no choice but to buy millions of copies of the best records. Sure, you could loan one to a friend, but they'd have to return it eventually, right? Blank records that could be recorded onto weren't a thing the average consumer could afford, so the music was protected, so to speak.

In the late 70s, Phillips brought to market an item that would forever change the musical landscape. The cassette, as it came to be known, relied on magnetic tape inside a casing, rather than the grooves of an LP. A much smaller medium, cassettes became hugely popular with the introduction of portable cassette players, most notably the Walkman. The music industry embraced cassette tapes, and the market was split pretty much evenly between LPs and cassettes for a while.

But all was not well in cassette land. As an open standard, development of the cassette was allowed by anyone who was interested, and Japanese cassette recorders, along with blank tapes, soon flooded the market. Recordable cassettes meant that people could copy their LPs (and other cassettes) to a blank tape, removing the need for consumers to purchase a copy of their own.

This, of course, became a hugely popular thing to do. Cassettes were cheap, less than a dollar each in most cases, and could be recorded on over and over again. People recorded their favorite songs off the radio, off their friends' records, and even from the air around them at concerts. Needless to say, the record companies were not happy. They sued virtually everyone they could. Of course, Pandora already opened the box – there was no going back. The record companies tried to appeal to the average music fan's sense of morality with a huge ad campaign:

This, as you can imagine, didn't do anything to stem the tide. After a while, things calmed down, and the record industry was fine. Music sales were the highest they'd ever been.

As the 1980s gave way to the 1990s, an even newer format came into popular use: the compact disc. Cheap to manufacture, but offering (for the first time) crystal clear digital sound, the record industry converted virtually their entire business to the CD within a few years. While people still could (and did) copy the music contained on CDs to blank cassettes, there was no way for the average consumer to make their own CDs, so people who copied the music would be getting a pale imitation of the CDs crystal clear sound. All was well.

If you haven't guessed by now, the computer revolution of the mid to late 1990s added CD (and then DVD) drives to millions of American households. Blank CDs were even cheaper than cassettes, costing only pennies each. People began to copy each other's CDs in record numbers, creating perfect digital replicas of store-bought CDs.

This time, the record industry didn't bother to freak out. They'd weathered this kind of storm twice before, and hadn't suffered any lasting ill-effects. This time was different.

As computers became more powerful, people began to take the CDs they purchased from the store and make digital copies on their computers, eschewing the blank CD entirely. In the late 1990s, the MP3 became the file format of choice for this "ripped" music. The concurrent rise of the Internet made music piracy a global phenomenon. People began to trade and collect MP3s as fast as their connections would allow. Then, in 1999, a bomb went off. The bomb was named Napster.

Developed by a well-meaning college kid named Shawn Fanning, Napster was a peer-to-peer networking application that allowed people to share their entire MP3 collections with the entire world. At its peak, over 100 million people were using the service to download and upload MP3s of everything from pre-release copies of major albums to old and out-of-print music unavailable anywhere else.

The record industry sued, musicians sued, pretty much everybody sued. This time they won, shutting down Napster in 2001. But it was a pyrrhic victory – dozens of other services followed in Napster's footsteps, making sure that the MP3 was here to stay. People, it turned out, were not about to give up on the convenience of digital music.

Right around this time, Apple CEO Steve Jobs had a grand vision for his company, centered on this new world of digital content. The MP3 was still steadily gaining in popularity, even inspiring some (terrible) portable players. These devices, notably the Creative Nomad and the Archos Jukebox, were clunky devices with limited battery life and absolutely appalling user interfaces.

Despite the objections and protestations of the record companies, Apple worked steadily (and secretly) on a device of their own for a couple of years. In late 2001, they unleashed the first iPod upon the world, immediately capturing the hearts and minds of millions of Apple devotees. Billed as "1,000 songs in your pocket", the original iPod was everything that its (long-forgotten) competitors were not: sleek, simple to use, and easy to manage.

The management part was taken care of by iTunes, an Apple program designed to help organize consumers' growing MP3 collections. Users (initially limited only to Apple-produced Macintosh computers) could even convert their existing CDs to the MP3 format at the touch of a button, copy them to their iPod, and voila! 1,000 songs were in your pocket. A copy of iTunes came pre-installed on every computer Apple sold from that point on, helping to make sure that everyone, even people who weren't already onboard with MP3s, had the power at their fingertips.

An innovative ad campaign followed, cementing the iPod as the "it" device of the decade before Windows users could even buy it for themselves.

Capitalizing on the success of the iPod, Apple continued to release new iterations of it – the iPod mini, the iPod Nano, the iPod Shuffle. To go along with all of these new devices, they began refining iTunes like crazy, moving from version 1.0 to 7.0 in just a few years.

Along the way, they convinced the (now desperate) record companies that they could help them sell music, rather than just be a receptacle for pirated MP3s. After securing permission, they added the iTunes Music Store, where people could purchase MP3 files for $.99 each, or entire albums for $9.99. By integrating the purchase into the software, Apple taught a whole generation of people that purchasing music was still the right thing to do.

The iPod also created an entirely new art form: the podcast. A portmanteau of 'iPod' and 'Broadcast', podcasts are sort of like radio shows, released to iTunes whenever a podcaster likes, on a subscription basis. We'll discuss the awesome-sauce that is the podcasting world a little later in this guide.

From this point, the story becomes a little more familiar. Apple would go on to practically own the digital media world, selling consumers everything from music to television shows, with books, movies, and apps thrown in for good measure. The iPhone and the iPad took the iPod concept and ran with it – first for the telephone, then for the touch screen tablet. But everything still comes back to the iPod, the idea that started it all. That's where the iPod Classic fits in – it's the only device left that stays true to the original.

What's in the Box (and what isn't)

As with all Apple products, your new iPod Classic is encased in some pretty beautiful packaging. Pretty much exactly the same as the packaging for the various iPhone models, you'll be given a cardboard box with a life-size picture of your model (color and all) on the top. Inside, you'll find several items:

- The iPod Classic itself (Black or Silver, 160GB)
- Ear Buds
- A 30 Pin to USB connector
- A 'Quick Start' guide and an Apple sticker
- A weird little piece of plastic that you'll never use (it's actually a 'Dock Adapter' for various iPod-friendly stereo systems)

Now, this is pretty much everything you'll need to get started, with two small exceptions. You might want to pick up these (relatively) low-cost items to complete the experience.

The first item you might want to pick up to get the most out of your iPod Classic is a set of headphones with player controls on them. Apple sells a version of these, and also includes them with their iPhone and iPod Touch devices. These headphones look almost identical to the ear buds included with your iPod Classic, but they have a small piece of plastic that looks like this:

This can be used to raise and lower the volume, change songs, play and pause the device, and pretty much anything else you can do with the iPod Classic. This can come in handy when using the device on the go, while jogging, or even at the gym. Check out Apple.com or Amazon for pricing, but a set of headphones with player controls shouldn't set you back more than 10 bucks.

These headphones also include a small built-in microphone, which will come in handy later in this guide when we discuss creating voice memos.

The second thing that's not included in the iPod Classic packaging is a USB wall charger. While the USB port on any computer is suitable for charging the device, plugging it into an outlet will charge the device in about half the time, which can be awfully convenient. Of course, we can't fault Apple for this omission, as wall chargers tend to be awfully big, and most consumers already have one or two of them in their home. The wall charger for any other device (like Amazon's Kindle, for example) will work just fine with the iPod Classic. If you don't happen to have one, there are (again) options for a dollar or two on sites like Amazon.com or even in most electronics stores.

The last, and perhaps least obvious, thing that's missing within the iPod Classic packaging is the software needed to use it. We'll get to the downloading and installation of iTunes a little later in this guide. For now, let's dig a little deeper and discuss the iPod Classic hardware.

The iPod Classic Hardware

As you can see from the above illustration, there are several components to the iPod Classic hardware. While we'll go over the specific functions of all this stuff a little later in this guide, let's take a second to learn a little bit about it before diving in.

The very bottom of your device is where the dock connector is. This is where you'll plug your cable in to connect it to your computer. Many third party devices (like stereos and car docks) also take advantage of this connector.

The front of your iPod Classic is dominated by a circular control system dubbed the 'Click Wheel'. This is basically a refinement of the control scheme that debuted with the original iPod. The screen above it is not touch-enabled, so we'll be navigating our way around the device exclusively through this Click Wheel apparatus.

The top of the iPod Classic has two parts to it: the hold button and the headphone jack. You'll plug your headphones into the headphone jack to listen to your iPod. Moving the hold button to the right (until you see orange) will disable the click wheel, allowing you to put the device in your pocket without worrying about accidentally pressing a button.

As for the click wheel, it's made up of five distinct buttons:

- Menu – pressing this will open the iPod Classic's menu system. More on that later.
- Previous/Rewind – pressing this will navigate to the previous song. Pressing and holding this will rewind within the current song.
- Play/Pause – pressing this once will begin playing the highlighted item. Pressing it a second time will pause the currently playing item.

- Next/Fast Forward – pressing this will navigate to the next song. Pressing and holding this will fast forward within the currently playing song.
- Center Button – this is the 'enter' button of the click wheel system. It's used to select items within menus and playlists. More on that a little later.

As for the actual 'wheel' portion of the click wheel, it's a touch-sensitive tool for scrolling through things. To scroll with the click wheel, just lightly place your finger on any part of the circle and move up or down in a concentric motion. You'll understand a little better when you begin using it, but for now, this illustration of how to scroll using this click wheel should suffice:

For now, let's begin preparing for our first use of the iPod Classic by downloading iTunes, the software we'll be using to manage the device.

Ready? Let's do this!

Part Two: Working With iTunes

Downloading/Installing iTunes

Before we get started using the iPod Classic, we'll have to set up the program that allows us to use the device with our computer. Users of Apple computers have the luxury of a pre-installed version of iTunes on their systems. For the rest of us, we've got to install it ourselves. While the rest of this guide is basically applicable to both operating systems, this particular section is just for the Windows folks.

While many (maybe even most) companies will include the software in the box the hardware came in, Apple does not share this philosophy. A lot of the relative sparseness inside your average package from Apple is meant as a nod to their "green" initiatives. After all, if you've bought a device that you're going to connect to your computer anyway, why include a CD that you might not use? To that end, in order to get started with iTunes, we're going to have to head to the Internet.

Even though iTunes is required to interact with our iPod Classic, there's a whole lot more to the program than that. ITunes also includes a built-in music store and access to both Podcasts and educational content from iTunes U, which we'll discuss a little later in this guide.

First things first: there are some basic minimum requirements your computer needs to meet in order to even *run* the iTunes software. While most modern computers will almost definitely pass muster, you should probably make sure before going ahead. Here's what your computer needs to *run* iTunes:

- 1Ghz or faster processor
- At least 512MB of ram
- A DirectX 9.0 compatible video card
- A monitor with a resolution of at least 1024x768

Now, there are a few additional things that, while not exactly requirements, are pretty much essential for getting any use out of iTunes. In order to play HD video or use iTunes LP or iTunes Extras, you'll need to have the following:

- 2Ghz Core 2 Duo (or faster) processor
- At least 1GB of ram (2GB for 1080p video)
- Intel GMA 3000 (or better) video card
- A 16 bit sound card w/ speaker
- A broadband Internet Connection

Now, you'll also have to be using a relatively modern version of Windows to install iTunes. You'll have to upgrade if you're not using *at least* Windows XP with Service Pack 2. Seeing as how that operating system is over 10 years old at this point, we'll go ahead and assume that this doesn't apply to very many people at this point.

Now that we've made sure our computer equipment is up to snuff, let's get down to business. To get started with installing iTunes 11, point your web browser to www.itunes.com. Once you've done that, you'll be greeted with this screen:

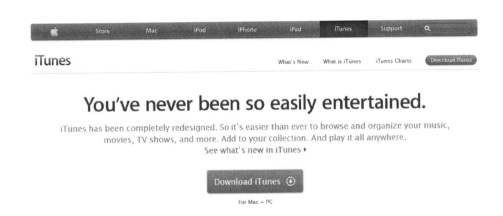

From here, all you need to do is click the blue box labeled 'Download iTunes'. Once you've done that, you'll be taken to a second screen with some more details. That will look like this:

As you can see, the website automatically detected which version of Windows we were using. This works 90% of the time, but it's a good idea to double check that you're downloading the 64

bit version if you're using a 64 bit version of Windows. To do this, just right click on the 'computer' icon in any explorer window to bring up the system information. You'll find either 32-bit or 64-bit operating system under the heading 'system type'.

As you can see, Apple would like to add your email address to a couple different mailing lists. Normally we'd tell you to go ahead and uncheck those boxes – but Apple does frequently run some pretty stunning sales on iTunes, and you'll likely miss them if you don't get the emails. We'll leave it up to you.

Once you've done that, click the blue box labeled 'Download Now' to begin downloading the iTunes software. It's a little under 90 megabytes in size, which should only take a couple of minutes on a standard broadband internet connection.

Depending on your web browser, you may have to give permission to download the application. Once you've done that, you'll find it wherever your web browser puts downloaded files, which is usually (but not always!) in the 'downloads' folder. If you're having trouble finding the file, just open the start menu and search for it. The file will be named either iTunes32setup.exe or iTunes64setup.exe and it'll look like this within the explorer window:

Once you've found the file, double-click it to open it and begin the installation process. Depending on your security settings, you'll probably have to give Windows permission to open the program. This permission request will come in the form of a pop-up window that looks like this:

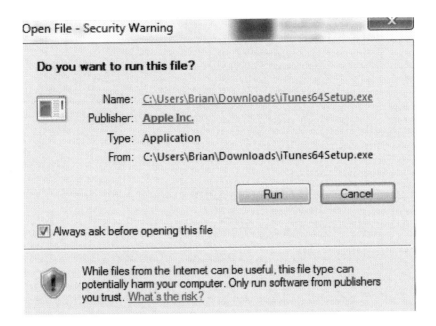

We can obviously trust Apple not to send us viruses, so go ahead and click 'run' to continue. Once you've done that, the setup program will begin its preparations. Hang back for a minute while it runs through this screen:

Once it's finished, you'll be greeted with the 'Welcome to iTunes' installer screen. This screen only exists as a chance to stop the installation. Tap 'Next' to proceed.

Once you've done that, you'll be presented with the 'installation options' screen. Here, you have a couple of options. You can choose to add a shortcut to iTunes on your desktop (go ahead, unless you're a desktop neat freak), make iTunes the default player for all of your audio files (this doesn't actually seem to work, so we'll have to it ourselves in the next section anyway).

You'll also be given a choice between automatically updating iTunes or doing it yourself (manually). On this point, we recommend unchecking that box. From time to time, an update will have bugs that haven't been worked out yet – we think it's better to update iTunes ourselves, after making sure that everything is copacetic.

Once you've made your decisions, click 'install' to initiate the installation process. Be patient – it'll take a few minutes. During the wait, Apple will display a couple of images touting various iTunes features. Just hang back and let it do its thing.

After a few minutes, you'll be greeted with the 'installation complete' screen:

From here, you can choose whether or not to open iTunes immediately after exiting the installer. Go ahead and leave that box checked, as we'll be diving right in to the software. Click 'finish' to complete the installation and launch iTunes.

That's all there is to it.

Setting Everything Up/The iTunes 11 Interface

Now that we've installed the iTunes 11 software and clicked 'finished', iTunes will automatically open for the first time. Before we can really dive in to the program, we have to go through a few more hurdles. First up: the iTunes Software License Agreement. This should pop up automatically a second or two after we click 'finish'.

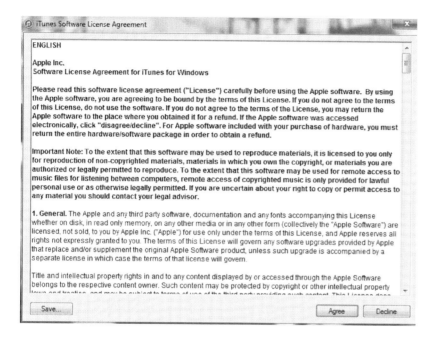

As you can see, there's a whole lot of reading to do. We'd *like* to say that every word of this is crucial for you to understand, but the truth is that it's just boilerplate legal mumbo-jumbo. You can just tap 'agree' and move on.

> *How do we know this? We actually wasted a half-hour of our lives reading through the entire thing. We might actually be the first to have ever done so. Trust us, it's not a thrilling read, and you're not missing anything.*

Once you've clicked 'agree', you'll (more than likely) be greeted with the following pop-up:

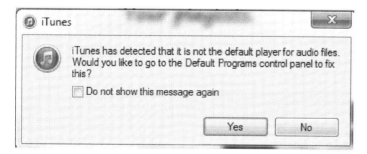

As you can see, iTunes is *not* actually the default player for audio files, despite the fact that we checked the appropriate box when installing the software. It's confusing – and maybe a little annoying – but don't worry; it's an easy fix. Just tap 'Yes' to set this feature up.

Once you've done that, you'll be greeted with the default programs menu. Find the menu item labeled 'select all' in the middle of the screen. Once you've done that, click 'save'. *Now* we've set iTunes as the default player for audio files.

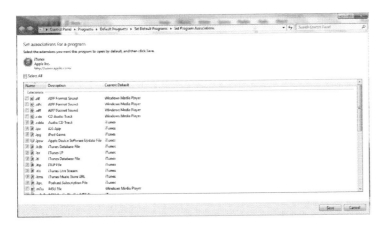

Once you've finished with that, you'll be greeted with yet another pop-up from iTunes. This time, you're simply giving permission for Apple to look through whatever MP3s you have in order to sort them and automatically retrieve album covers and other info, saving you a little legwork. Just click 'agree' to let this happen.

Once you've done that, you'll be given the opportunity to either enter the iTunes store or begin scanning for the music on your hard drive. We'll go over the iTunes store a little later in this guide, so for right now, just let iTunes scan your hard drive. Depending on how much music you're storing on your computer, this might take a few minutes.

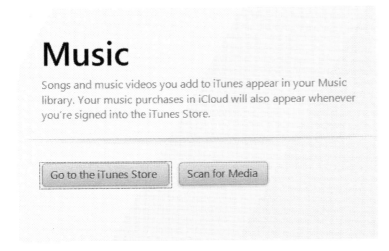

Once that's finished, you're all set up. All that's left to do is navigate our way around the iTunes 11 interface. To get started, let's first take a look at the top of the program screen. This is where we'll be doing most of our navigating from.

As you can see, there are several parts to this interface. First, let's discuss that little box in the corner. This is where the traditional *file, edit, etc.* menu system usually seen in Windows programs resides. Click it once to take a look at what's inside.

- New – this area is where playlists are created. We'll go over playlists in a later section of this guide.
- Library – this area is reserved for home sharing and manually downloading album artwork.
- ITunes Store—this is where we'll interact with our iTunes account, including the authorization of our various computers and devices.
- Add File to Library – for files you'd like to manually add to the iTunes library after the initial search that we just performed, this is where we'll do that.
- Get Info – this menu item is context dependent. If you've selected an item within iTunes, you'll be able to get its information, and edit it if you choose. More on that a little later.
- Switch to MiniPlayer – iTunes comes with a smaller, unobtrusive player, for use when you're doing other things with your computer. Clicking here will activate it.
- Preferences – this section contains all of the advanced features and settings for iTunes 11. We'll get in-depth with this in a moment.
- Show Menu Bar – click here to activate the traditional Windows-style *file, edit, view* type menu system. It's a good idea to enable that now, as we'll be going over it shortly.
- Exit – clicking here will exit the iTunes 11 program.

Now, below the little box in the corner, you'll see an icon that's labeled 'Music'. Click it, and you'll see that it expands to include four selectable categories: Music, Movies, TV Shows, and Home Sharing.

These items are, in essence, your library of content. Since we've only just started the program, the only library that will have any content in it will be your Music library, which is now full of whatever music was on your hard drive that iTunes automatically detected. Below the Library Menu, you'll find all of your content, which will look something like this:

On the right hand side of the screen, you'll find a button labeled 'iTunes Store'. Clicking here will switch the program's functionality from media player to media store, and clicking it again will switch it back. But let's not get ahead of ourselves. Before we explore the iTunes Store, we'll have to set it up.

Ready? Let's go!

Part Three: Using iTunes

The iTunes Store

Now that we've learned a little bit about the iTunes 11 interface, let's go ahead and set up the iTunes Store so we can begin browsing for new content to add. This section primarily applies to folks who've never had an iTunes account – those who have can simply sign in and skip the following tutorial.

To get started with the iTunes Store, go ahead and click the 'iTunes Store' button on the upper right hand side of the program. Once you do, the interface will now look something like this:

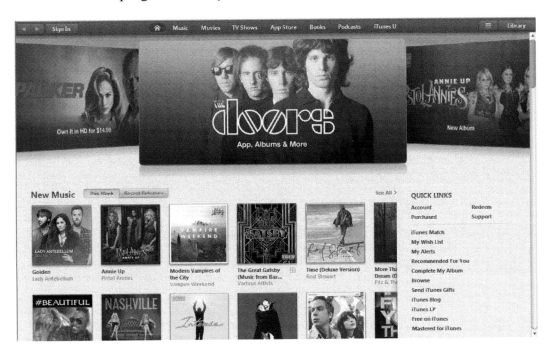

In the upper left-hand corner of the screen, you'll now find a button labeled 'Sign In'. Tap it to begin the account creation process. You'll be greeted with a pop-up screen that looks like this:

If you've already got an Apple ID, great. Just sign in and you're done. For those who don't, however, click the button on the bottom left that's labeled 'Create Apple ID'. Once you've done that, you'll be taken back to the main window of the iTunes 11 program, which will now look like this:

With an Apple ID, you can download the latest music, videos, and more.

To begin creating your Apple ID, click Continue.

*In previous versions of iTunes, all of these various screens that appear within the main window were actually separate things. This new emphasis on 'unification' makes things a lot simpler than in previous iterations. Lucky us!

Click 'Continue' to begin the process of creating an Apple ID. Once you've done that, you'll be presented with yet another 'Terms and Conditions' page that you'll have to agree to. Check the box labeled 'I have read and agree to the terms and conditions' and click 'Continue' again.

Once you've done that, you'll be greeted with a page full of details to fill out, including an email address, a password, and answers to a few 'security questions' in case you ever get locked out of your account. This is mostly like anything else you've ever signed up for online, with one major exception: the password requirements are a little bit, shall we say, strict. It took us a few tries to land on a password that Apple approved of. In fact, here's their list of rules for the initial password you create:

Password must:

- ○ Have at least one letter
- ○ Have at least one capital letter
- ○ Have at least one number
- ● Not contain multiple identical consecutive characters
- ● Not be the same as the account name
- ○ Be at least 8 characters

In short, Apple *really* cares about the security of your account. Once you've created your bulletproof password and entered in the rest of the information, click 'Continue' to be taken to the payment method page. Enter your credit card (or PayPal) information and your billing address, and click 'Create Apple ID' to finish the process.

Once that's done, you'll be automatically logged into your iTunes account. You'll see your account ID in the left hand corner of the screen:

Click here at any time to look at (or edit) your account details, sign out, or redeem iTunes gift cards.

Now that we've set up our iTunes account, let's take a look at how everything works. Remember, any time you'd like to return to your library, just click that same button in the right hand corner of the screen, which is now labeled – appropriately enough – 'Library'.

As we touched on briefly a little earlier in this guide, you can now see the seven mini-stores that make up the iTunes Store. They're right there along the top of the screen, next to the icon that looks like a house. Clicking this 'Home' icon will take you to a sort of overview of all the stores. This is mostly just advertising for the 'featured' items in each store, but it gives a good overview of the sheer breadth of content available.

In addition to these items, you'll find some helpful stuff along the right hand side. Here, you'll see various iTunes Charts – the most purchased/downloaded items in the store.

8. **Life On a Rock**
   Kenny Chesney

9. **Mother**
   Natalie Maines

10. **The Heist (Deluxe Edition)**
    Macklemore & Ryan Lewis

TOP MOVIES >

1. **Jack Reacher**
   Action & Adventure

2. **Silver Linings Playbook**
   Comedy

3. **Safe Haven (2013)**
   Drama

4. **Django Unchained**
   Action & Adventure

5. **Parker**
   Action & Adventure

TOP TV SHOWS >

Seasons   Episodes

1. **Mad Men**
   Season 6

Clicking on any of the specific mini-store labels at the top will limit the store to *just* that content, giving you a more detailed overview of what's available. Clicking on any item within the store will bring up that item's details. For example, we clicked on "Push the Sky Away", the new album from the critically acclaimed group Nick Cave and the Bad Seeds. We were greeted with this page:

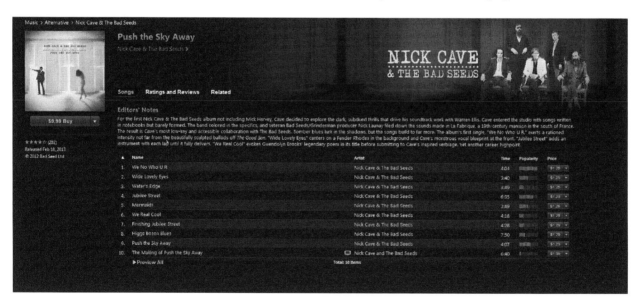

As you can see, there's a *ton* of information here. This is the case for pretty much every album in the entire catalog. You'll see a brief description under the heading 'Editors Notes' as well as the track listing in the middle of the screen. Each individual song can be previewed by clicking the track number. Once clicked, the track will immediately begin to play in iTunes without leaving the page. For most songs, you'll be given a 90 second preview.

To the right of each track, you'll see a link to purchase the individual songs. While this is true for most albums in the iTunes catalog, some songs from some artists are labeled 'album only' and cannot be previewed or purchased individually.

Single songs can be purchased for $1.29, while full albums are generally a little bit cheaper than the sum of the tracks. Interestingly, iTunes will give you the option to 'complete your album' by purchasing the rest of the tracks for the difference in price between what you've already purchased and the price of the album. In the example above, we could purchase a single song at $1.29, and then later purchase the rest of the album for only $8.70.

Once you've purchased an item, it will begin downloading immediately. As soon as it's finished, it will appear within your iTunes library, ready to use and copy over to your iPod Classic.

In the next section, we'll begin to use the iPod Classic, copy some music to it, and discuss some of its more advanced features.

Ready? Let's do it!

Part Four: Using iPod Classic

Connecting your iPod Classic for the First Time

Now that we've installed (and learned a bit about) iTunes, it's time to begin using the iPod Classic. To get started, plug the USB cable into an available USB port on your computer, and then plug the 30 pin end into the port on the bottom of your device.

The next couple of paragraphs assume that you're using a Windows computer. If you're using a Mac, just open iTunes after you've plugged in the device and follow along from there.

Once you've done that, you'll be greeted with the 'installing device driver' bubble in the bottom right corner of your desktop:

This is Windows figuring out what you've just plugged in. Once it's finished, you'll be greeted with this pop-up:

Click 'close' to finish the installation process. ITunes should automatically open at this point. If it doesn't, just launch the program from the start menu. Once you've done that, you'll be shown the new iPod setup screen, which will look like this:

Click 'continue' to begin.

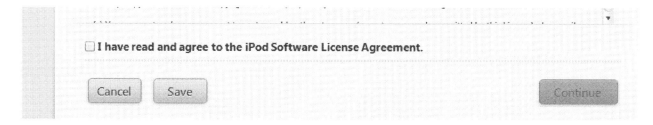

□ I have read and agree to the iPod Software License Agreement.

Cancel   Save   Continue

The first thing you'll have to do is agree to the terms and conditions (again). Click the check box and tap 'continue' to move on. Once you've done that, you'll be shown a quick walk-through page, covering the various ways you'll be interacting with the iPod Shuffle from within iTunes.

Click 'continue' to move on. You'll be greeted with another 'get started' page. Click 'Get Started' to move on.

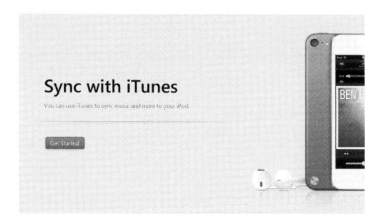

Once you've done that, you'll be taken to the iPod Classic summary page.

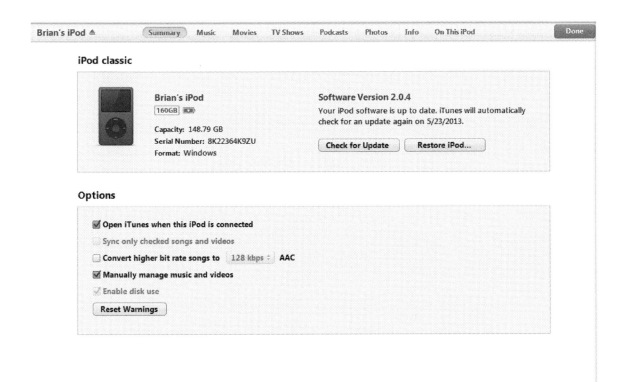

From here, you have a few options. Near the top of the page, you can manually check for software updates, though Apple hasn't released one in a while, as the software functions pretty much perfectly. Next to that, you'll find the 'Restore iPod' button. Click here if you ever run into problems and need to reset your device. Bear in mind that this will reset the device to factory defaults, removing any trace of anything you may have copied to it.

this is also what you should do if you ever (god forbid!) want to sell the device to someone else.

Below that, you'll find the options menu. There are several items here:

- Open iTunes when this iPod is connected – this item is pretty self-explanatory. If you keep this box checked, iTunes will open every time you connect the iPod to your computer.
- Sync only checked songs and videos – we'll go over this in the next section.
- Convert higher bit rate songs to…-- this item is mostly reserved for iPod devices with limited storage. Checking this box will allow you to copy lower-quality copies of your music files to the iPod, while keeping the higher-quality ones in your iTunes library. If you're running low on space, this is a good option to look into.
- Manually manage music and videos – we'll go over this in the next section.
- Enable disk use – a lesser-known function of the iPod family, you can actually use your iPod like a USB flash drive by copying files to it in Windows Explorer. You won't be able to see these files in iTunes, but you can move them from computer to computer this way.

Adding Music to Your iPod Classic

Now that we've got our iPod Classic all set up with iTunes, it's time to start adding some music to the device. There are a few different ways to do this, all of them pretty easy to do.

From the 'Summary' view that we entered upon finishing the setup, find the button labeled 'Done' and click it. This will take us back to the library view.

As you can see, your library view is a little bit different now. In addition to the buttons for 'iTunes Store' and the various libraries, you'll now have an 'iPod' icon that looks like this:

Click that icon at any time to return to the iPod summary view.

Now that that's sorted, let's discuss the three main ways to get content onto your iPod.

Manually

The most common method for copying things to your iPod is to do it manually, a song or album at a time. It's also the simplest way. To copy a song manually, just click to highlight the song, and then drag it over to the right side of the screen:

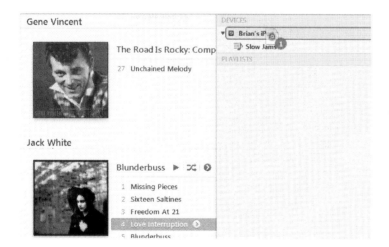

As you can see, a 'devices' pain will automatically open up on the right hand side of the screen. To copy a song to the iPod, just drag it to that device. You'll see a red number icon – this is to tell you how many songs you're currently copying over.

To copy an entire album to the iPod, just drag the album cover over to the right in the same way. As you can see, copying is the same as it is for a single song, with the exception of that red number. This time, the number is 13 – the number of songs on the album that we're copying over.

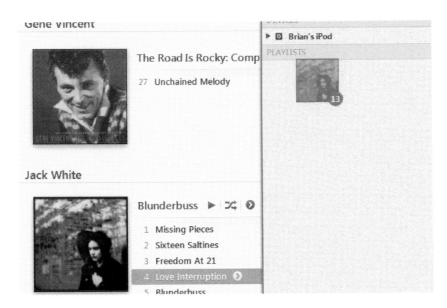

To copy a bunch of different songs all at once, just highlight one of the songs, and then press the CTRL button on your keyboard. Click to highlight any other songs you want to copy, all while continuing to hold the CTRL button. When you've highlighted everything you want to copy over, just drag one of the highlighted items to the right – all of the songs will copy over, giving you whatever amount you're copying as that magic red number:

Using Playlists

The playlist concept is one of the coolest features of iTunes. We've got a bunch of music in our library, ready to copy over to our iPod, but as we discussed earlier, every song you play will be followed by the next track on the album. What about those times when you want to listen to a mixture of a bunch of different stuff? Enter playlists.

Playlists are, in the simplest of terms, files that iTunes uses to create customized albums. You can create a playlist and fill it with any song in your library, in any order you choose. Once you begin playing a playlist, iTunes will play only the songs you've added, and only in the order you want. Pretty cool, huh? It's also shockingly easy to set up.

To get started with playlists, click the playlists tab on the library menu. Once you've done that, you'll be greeted with a screen that looks like this:

As you can see, playlists are kept on the left hand side, while the items within the playlist take up the middle of the screen. By default, there are six different playlists listed in this section. These are really just suggestions from Apple. To begin creating your own playlist, head to the bottom left of the screen. There you'll find a button labeled with the + symbol.

Click the + sign, and then click 'New Playlist'. Once you've done that, you'll be taken to the playlist creation screen.

The first thing you'll want to do is give the playlist a name. You can choose anything you like here, but it's generally a good idea to use something that's descriptive like "Slow Jams" or "Best of Bananarama".

Once you've decided on a name for your playlist, just click on any song in the main part of the screen and drag it to the right. Once you've done that, the song is added to the playlist. That's all there is to it.

To add multiple songs at one time, simply click on one song, press the ctrl button and click on the other songs you'd like to add. Once you've chosen all the songs you'd like to add, drag one to the right and all of the songs will be added.

Instead of dragging, you can also right-click on a selection, which will bring up this context menu:

From there, find the menu item labeled 'Add to Playlist' and choose the playlist you'd like to add the songs to. It's that simple.

Once you've added some songs, rearrange them into any order you like by dragging the files on the right up or down in the list:

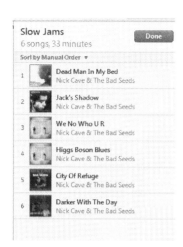

When you've finished creating your playlist, click 'done' to exit the playlist editor. Then, to copy the playlist to your iPod, just click into Playlist view, find your playlist and drag it to the right, just as you would a single song or album:

Drag it up to the iPod icon to copy the playlist to the device.

Syncing

If copying files and playlists over to your iPod seems like too much of a hassle, Apple does have an easier way. ITunes will allow you to sync *everything* in your library to any device, updating it as you add or delete files (and plug in the device). Since the iPod Classic comes standard with 160GB worth of storage space, this is a very convenient option for people with large libraries of music. Here's how to set it up:

Click the iPod icon to move to iPod Summary view:

Once you've done that, head to the 'options' section of the page, and find the item labeled 'Manually Manage Music and Videos'.

Uncheck the checkbox to change the iPod to syncing mode. Once you've done that, a pop-up window will show up, asking you to confirm.

Now, it's important to note that anything you've copied to the iPod will be deleted when you click 'ok'. If you're comfortable with that, go ahead and click.

From there, press the 'apply' button on the bottom of your screen.

Once you've done that, all of your music will begin to copy over to the device. You can choose to exclude certain things by clicking over to the 'music', 'Movies', 'TV Shows', 'Podcasts', or 'Photos' tabs within the iPod Summary view:

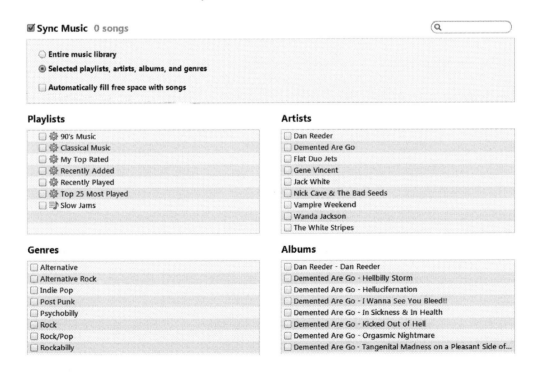

Click the checkbox next to 'Entire Music Library' to sync everything, or check each box individually to check only what you want, sorted by genre, artist, album, or playlist.

The iPod Classic Interface

Now that we've copied some music to our iPod Classic, let's take a look at the iPod Classic interface. To follow along, press the menu or center button on your device to wake up the screen.

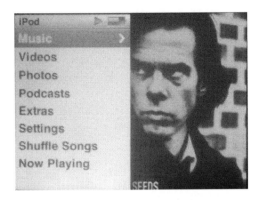

Now, when you first wake up the device, you'll be greeted with the iPod's 'Home' Screen. On the right half of the screen, you'll find random cover art for whatever you've copied to the device. This will change often. On the left hand side, you'll see the main menu, which is comprised of various folders for the different kinds of content that your iPod supports: Music, Videos, Photos, and Podcasts.

Scroll up and down by moving your finger around the click-wheel, as we discussed near the beginning of this guide. Click the center button to select an item.

Below that, you'll find the 'Extras' menu, which includes things like a clock, an alarm, a stopwatch, and a couple of random games.

Before the introduction of the iPhone, there were actually dozens of games available for the iPod Classic, sold on iTunes for around 5 bucks each. They've since been discontinued, but can be found for free as 'abandon ware' if you know where to look. It should be noted, however, that this could be illegal, and most of the games were nothing like the mobile games we've come to expect – that is, they aren't really any good.

Below that, you'll find the settings menu, which consists of the following items:

- About – clicking here will bring up a visual representation of how much of the iPod's space you've used so far, and what kind of items are taking up that space.
- Shuffle – clicking here will toggle off/on the shuffle function of the iPod. If this is turned on, your iPod will choose a random song from your collection to play, followed by more and more random songs until it's turned off.
- Repeat – clicking this once will turn repeat on for the selected playlist. Clicking it again will repeat the selected song. Clicking it a third time will turn the function off.
- Main Menu – clicking here will allow you to customize what shows up in the 'home' menu.
- Music Menu – clicking here will allow you to customize what shows up in the 'music' menu.
- Volume Limit – for legal reasons, your iPod doesn't get ear-crushingly loud by default. Click here to fix that problem and raise the limit to whatever you like.

- Backlight – click here to adjust how long the screen stays on.
- Brightness – click here to adjust how bright the screen gets.
- Audiobooks – click here to adjust how fast audiobooks play. This is something you probably shouldn't mess with, as it makes things sound incredibly weird.
- EQ – your iPod comes with a built-in equalizer. Turn it on/off from here, and adjust the sound to your liking. Bear in mind that this will diminish how long the battery lasts.
- Sound Check – the iPod Classic also has a built-in 'normalizing' function. Clicking here will turn it on, making all of your music play at the same level, regardless of how loud the original recording is.
- Clicker – clicking here will turn off/on the clicking sound that's heard whenever you use the click wheel.
- Date and Time – adjust date and time settings here.
- Sort By – click here to adjust how your contacts are sorted (if you decide to use contacts)
- Language – click here to change the default language that your iPod's menu system uses.
- Legal – a mobile version of all the legal mumbo-jumbo from iTunes.
- Reset Settings – click here to return all of these settings to the defaults. This won't delete your content, just the settings.

Now, within the Music menu, there are several ways to get to the songs you want to hear.

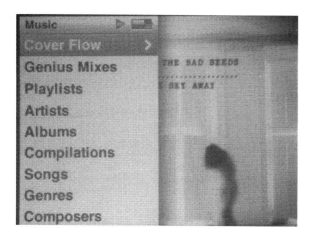

As you can see from the above illustration, all of your music can be sorted in different ways. You can click any of the submenus to find the same content, but sorted a bit differently. Cover flow, for example, is a scrollable list of all of your albums in a visual way:

Scroll from left to right or vice versa. When you've found the album you're looking for, tap the center button or the play/pause button to begin playing the album.

The 'Albums' item is the same, except without the fancy artwork:

The 'Artists' view will sort everything by the artist, then by album within that:

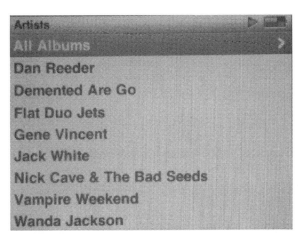

Of course, you can also copy any playlists you've created to the iPod. These will be viewable, appropriately enough, under the 'Playlists' menu:

Notice the playlist labeled 'On-The-Go' in your playlist list? This is a little-used, but awfully cool feature of your iPod Classic. It's a built-in playlist that you can add to straight from the device. To use the On-The-Go playlist, just begin playing a song you'd like to add. Hold down the center button for a few seconds and a menu will pop up. Click 'Add to On-The-Go' to add the song to your playlist.

Working with Video

In addition to its top-notch music function, your iPod Classic also functions as a video player. While the screen isn't exactly the largest thing available, it works better than you'd think.

The one caveat: the devices meant to work with iTunes (like the iPod Classic) will only play video files in one specific format called MPEG-4 (MP4 or M4V). While the videos sold in the iTunes store are always in this format, most videos downloaded or purchased elsewhere are not. Apple hasn't yet allowed iTunes to convert these files automatically, as they have with audio files, leaving those of you with other formats (like AVI or MKV) with no easy way of transferring this content to iTunes, and then to your iPod.

We can get around this in two ways. First, we can simply purchase all of our content through iTunes. This can get expensive pretty quickly. The second, and slightly more complicated method, is to take our existing DVDs (or AVI files) and convert them using third-party software.

There are a few options out there that will help you, but the gold standard is a free, open source piece of software called 'Handbrake'. While a full tutorial of the program is beyond the scope of this guide, there is a handy guide to all of this located at www.handbrake.fr. The rest of this section will assume that you've either purchased some iTunes video content or converted some of your own.

To copy video files to your iPod Classic, head to the 'Movies' or 'TV Shows' library in iTunes. Once there, find the video file(s) you'd like to copy over. Click once to highlight the file, and then drag the file to the right hand side of the screen. Just like with audio files, a separate section will show up, including an icon for your iPod. Drag the file up to the iPod icon, and note the red number.

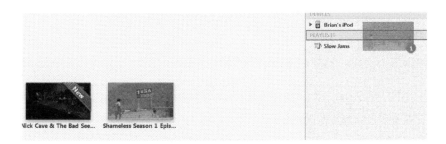

Nick Cave & The Bad See...   Shameless Season 1 Epis...

Once you've copied the video file to your iPod, it will be viewable from the 'Videos' menu, separated by Movies, TV Shows, Rentals, and Music Videos. Click on it to begin playing. The controls for the video work in exactly the same way as they do for audio.

Podcasts: An Overview

As we touched on briefly at the beginning of this guide, there is a wealth of free content available through iTunes that you can copy over to your iPod whenever you like. The most celebrated, and for good reason, is probably the podcast. ITunes practically invented the market for podcasts, and it shows. Let's take a quick look at how this works.

Podcasts can be anything from news programs to comedy shows, and everything in between. It's helpful to think of podcasts as the modern-day equivalent to the old time radio show, which encompassed everything from horror stories to Little Orphan Annie. Basically, anything you can serialize qualifies, and iTunes has *thousands* of them.

Podcasts have their own iTunes mini-store. It's kind of a misnomer, as the podcasts in the store are free to download. Organizing it in store form, however, makes it really easy to browse and find the content you're looking for.

To get started with podcasts, click the iTunes Store button and then the Podcasts tab. Once you've done that, you'll be greeted with a page that looks something like this:

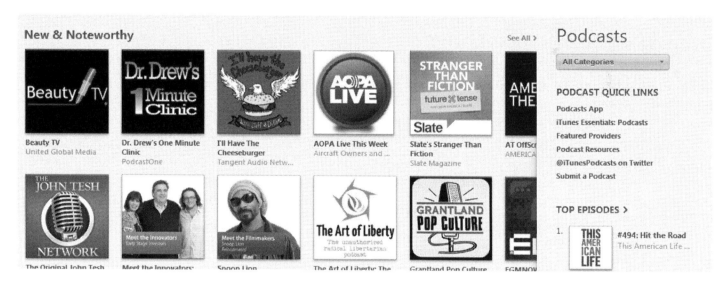

Feel free to browse the store in the same way you have previously for music and movies. It functions in the same way. You can also enter anything you like in the search bar or click the 'all categories' dropdown menu for a list of various podcast categories.

While most of the podcasts are audio only, some are video. You'll notice the video podcasts have a little icon next to them that looks a lot like a television. Once you've landed on something you'd like to check out, click on it to be taken to that podcast's page. For our example, we clicked on the *hugely* popular podcast "WTF with Marc Maron", a comedy/interview show that's updated twice a week.

As you can see, it's set up a lot like an album page in the music section of the iTunes store. There are tabs for details, ratings and reviews, and related items. On the left, you'll see track numbers. Hovering over these track numbers will bring up a play button. While in the music iTunes Store, this would play a 90 second preview of the track, in the podcast section it'll play the entire thing. To "purchase" individual episodes, click on the label 'free' on the right side of each track. Once you've done that, the episode will immediately begin downloading.

Alternately, you can also click the button labeled 'Subscribe' just below the podcast's picture. This will bring up the subscription dialog box:

As you can see, clicking subscribe will download the latest episode of the podcast, and then automatically download all future episodes as they are released. This is pretty convenient, saving you the trouble of searching for a podcast every time you want to download another episode.

Once you've downloaded at least one podcast, your library will now have a separate section for them:

To access your podcasts, just select the 'Podcasts' item in the library menu. Once you've done that, you'll be greeted with the podcast library screen, which will look something like this:

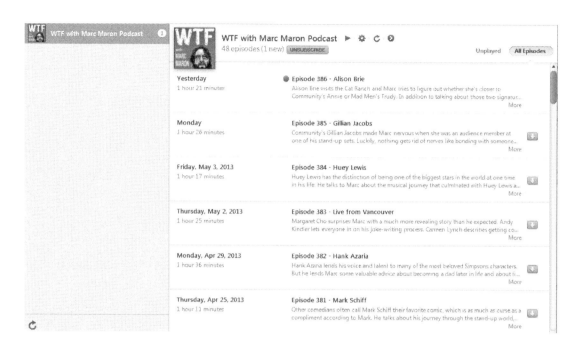

From there, you can simply drag the episode(s) you want to listen to toward the right side of the screen to copy them to your iPod. You can also sync the podcast to your device by tabbing over to the podcast view' on your iPod summary page and clicking 'Sync Podcasts'

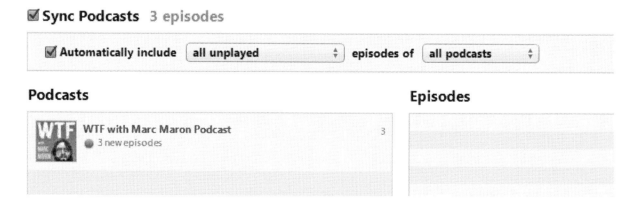

This will copy all new, un-played episodes of your podcasts to your device whenever it's plugged in. From there, you'll find them under the 'Podcasts' menu on your iPod Classic.

Conclusion

So there you have it. The iPod Classic, while Apple's oldest current product, is a pretty amazing device. We've shown you all that you need to know – how to work with iTunes, how to copy your music and video files to the device, and even how to create playlists. We've introduced you to the magical world of podcasts. You're truly ready to get the most out of your iPod Classic. We're sure you'll get years of enjoyment out of it.

We hope you've enjoyed reading this guide as much as we've enjoyed writing it. We hope that we've given you the tools to not only use (and love) your iPod Classic, but to treat any tech gadget the way you should – not as something to be afraid of, but as something to explore, play with, and master.

Thanks for reading!

About Minute Help Press

Minute Help Press is building a library of books for people with only minutes to spare. Follow @minutehelp on Twitter to receive the latest information about free and paid publications from Minute Help Press, or visit minutehelpguides.com.

Printed in Great Britain
by Amazon